WEEKLY WR READER®

EARLY LEARNING LIBRARY

+ SAFETY FIRST

Staying Safe
On My Bike

by Joanne Mattern

Reading consultant: Susan Nations, M.Ed.,
author/literacy coach/consultant in literacy development

Please visit our web site at: www.garethstevens.com
For a free color catalog describing Weekly Reader® Early Learning Library's list
of high-quality books, call 1-877-445-5824 (USA) or 1-800-387-3178 (Canada).
Weekly Reader® Early Learning Library's fax: (414) 336-0164.

Library of Congress Cataloging-in-Publication Data

Mattern, Joanne, 1963-
    Staying safe on my bike / by Joanne Mattern.
      p. cm. — (Safety first)
    Includes bibliographical references and index.
    ISBN-13: 978-0-8368-7794-6 (lib. bdg.)
    ISBN-13: 978-0-8368-7801-1 (softcover)
    1. Cycling—Safety measures—Juvenile literature.   2. Safety education—
Juvenile literature. I. Title.
    GV1055.M4   2007
    796.60289—dc22   2006030336

This edition first published in 2007 by
Weekly Reader® Early Learning Library
A Member of the WRC Media Family of Companies
330 West Olive Street, Suite 100
Milwaukee, WI 53212 USA

Copyright © 2007 by Weekly Reader® Early Learning Library

Managing editor: Valerie J. Weber
Editor: Barbara Kiely Miller
Art direction: Tammy West
Cover design and page layout: Charlie Dahl
Picture research: Diane Laska-Swanke
Photographer: Jack Long

The publisher thanks Phillip, Anna, and Doreen Martinez; Timmy Emanuelson; and
Brady and Robert Kraus for their assistance with this book.

Printed in the United States of America

1 2 3 4 5 6 7 8 9 10 10 09 08 07 06

Note to Educators and Parents

Reading is such an exciting adventure for young children! They are beginning to integrate their oral language skills with written language. To encourage children along the path to early literacy, books must be colorful, engaging, and interesting; they should invite the young reader to explore both the print and the pictures.

The *Safety First* series is designed to help young readers review basic safety rules, learn new vocabulary, and strengthen their reading comprehension. In simple, easy-to-read language, each book teaches children to stay safe in an everyday situation such as at home, school, or in the outside world.

Each book is specially designed to support the young reader in the reading process. The familiar topics are appealing to young children and invite them to read — and reread — again and again. The full-color photographs and enhanced text further support the student during the reading process.

In addition to serving as wonderful picture books in schools, libraries, homes, and other places where children learn to love reading, these books are specifically intended to be read within an instructional guided reading group. This small group setting allows beginning readers to work with a fluent adult model as they make meaning from the text. After children develop fluency with the text and content, the book can be read independently. Children and adults alike will find these books supportive, engaging, and fun!

— Susan Nations, M.Ed., author, literacy coach,
and consultant in literacy development

Do you like to ride your bike? Do you know how to ride safely?

First, sit on the seat. Can you reach the ground, the pedals, and the **handlebars**?

handlebars

pedal

Then, ask your parents to check the **tires**. Are they full of air?

tire

Always wear a bike **helmet**.
A helmet keeps your head
safe if you fall.

helmet

11

Always ride on the right side of the sidewalk or the street. Ride **single file**, one person behind the other.

sidewalk

Stop at stop signs. At stoplights, wait for the green light. Look both ways before going!

Let others know you want to turn. Hold your left arm straight out to show you are turning left.

Bend your left arm up to show you are turning right. Bend it down to show you are going to stop.

19

Watch out for other bike riders on a bike path, road, or sidewalk. Watch out for people walking, too! A good bike ride is a safe bike ride.

Glossary

handlebars — the bars on the front of a bike that you hold on to to steer

helmet — a hard hat that protects your head

single file — a line of people or things moving or standing one behind the other

tires — wheels

For More Information

Books

Bicycle Safety. Be Safe! (series). Peggy Pancella
   (Heinemann Library)

Bicycle Safety. Living Well, Safety (series). Lucia Raatma
   (Child's World)

On Your Bike. Safety First (series). Ruth Thomson (Franklin Watts)

Play It Safe. Mercer Mayer (McGraw-Hill Children's Publishing)

Web Sites

Bicycle Safety
www.state.il.us/kids/isp/bikes
Make sure you and your bike stay safe with these tips from the
Illinois State Police.

Safety on Wheels
ou.edu/oupd/kidsafe/bicycle.htm
This cartoon shows the rules you should follow for a safe bike ride.

Index

About the Author

Joanne Mattern has written more than 150 books for children. She has written about weird animals, sports, world cities, dinosaurs, and many other subjects. Joanne also works in her local library. She lives in New York State with her husband, three daughters, and assorted pets. She enjoys animals, music, going to baseball games, reading, and visiting schools to talk about her books.